REAL TALK ON A BLESSED DAY

*Just Keeping It Real
When So Many Others Are Afraid To*

by

STARLENE R. PATTERSON

Copyright © 2012 Starlene R. Patterson
All rights reserved.

ISBN: 0615672019
ISBN 13: 9780615672014

This book is dedicated to my dear friend of over twenty-five years, Ms. Sharon Holland. She was there for me in one of the darkest moments of my life when we were teenagers. She and her family always showed me love. Our friendship always remained strong, despite our periods of separation and silence. She is the person who inspired me to write this book.

Welcome to *Real Talk on a Blessed Day*. If you are ready to be honest with yourself and with others, then this book is for you. I had to be honest with myself and the shortcomings of my human nature before I could even attempt to put my thoughts into this book. I have experienced many of the things that I have written about at different stages of my life as I proceeded through my personal growth process. The few things that I didn't experience I learned from other people's experiences. A time comes in your life when you declare that you are not going to keep on going though things unnecessarily because I, for one, do not believe that experience is always the best teacher, but learning to listen is, and thus far it has become one of my greatest attributes. I have to reflect constantly on where I came from, where I am now, and where I am on my way to. I have made plenty of mistakes, but I thank God that I am not my mistakes. God has taught me how to turn my mistakes and past misery into a modern-day miracle that I can share with others. For I am a firm believer that nothing gets done alone, and when we are trying to navigate our lives, sometimes we need a helping hand, a shoulder to lean on, or just some words of encouragement. I strongly believe that, in some form, my inspirational journal is a combination of all three elements, and it's my prayer that as you read these short conversations, you will find hope, strength, and courage to continue to press on daily and never give up or in, no matter what challenges you face.

LET THE 365 DAY JOURNEY BEGIN

DAY 1

It's always a great feeling to celebrate each milestone in life, and it's definitely good to pat yourself on the back when others may not do it.

DAY 2

It's never good to envy someone else's success, especially if you don't want to do what he or she did to get there.

DAY 3

When you see a person in his or her moment of glory, keep in mind that you may not always know his or her entire story of struggles, pains, and setbacks that led to his or her ultimate comeback.

DAY 4

I firmly believe in celebrating the successes of life, whether they are big or small, mine or the next person's.

DAY 5

Anger is that natural emotion that should never be ignored. You can't run or hide from it. When anger goes unchecked, you can guarantee that self-destruction is soon to follow. It has broken up families, marriages, friends, lost jobs, etc. It is so powerful that it can immobilize a person. The best way to manage anger successfully is to exercise self-control and choose what you are going to entertain.

DAY 6

When a person uses words recklessly from misplaced anger, the damage done often cannot be repaired.

DAY 7

Words can never be taken back, and choosing them wisely when you are angry is hard to do. Walking away is also hard to do, but it's better than sticking around and losing control.

DAY 8

Your attitude is your thought life turned inside out, and if you listen closely to yourself, you will realize whether you need an attitude adjustment or not.

DAY 9

Negative attitude, negative results. Positive attitude, positive results.

DAY 10

No matter what is going on in your life, you must believe that you deserve the best, and you should never settle for less. Set the standard, go for what you know, and expect the best results.

DAY 11

No one gets it right 100 percent, and everyone at one point in life had

the doormat experience where people walked on top of them until they

came to their senses, realized that no one should have so much

power over them, and then set up boundaries.

DAY 12

I believe that you will teach people how to treat you by what you tolerate. Boundaries are necessary to keep people in check and to keep you from going too far.

DAY 13

If you truly value your life, then you will guard your privacy like Fort Knox. There are just too many things about people's lives on display that should be a kept a secret.

DAY 14

Let your yes be yes, your no be no, and don't feel bad about your decision.

DAY 15

No one has any power over you except for what you allow.

DAY 16

Our lives at times can be similar to an airplane that can carry only a certain amount of weight. If the plane has too much baggage on board, it will be ineffective, unable to soar, and will be stuck on the runway. Many times we exceed the weight limit in our lives by carrying too much baggage of burdens that aren't even ours. So make a decision to unload the unnecessary and give it to God, so you can soar in your own life.

DAY 17

Sometimes you have to pull the plug on people who drain you of your time and resources and who do not help you to prosper but, instead, pull you back to the place in your life you've worked hard to grow away from.

DAY 18

Sometimes we must realize our limitations by not carrying other peoples burdens that are meant only for God to carry. Don't get me wrong—it's okay to listen, make suggestions, or offer some temporary comfort, but to try to fix someone else's problem is just not our responsibility.

DAY 19

For every obstacle in life, there will always be an opportunity, and for every opportunity in life, there will always be an obstacle. Either way, do the best you can, and keep pressing forward until you reach that goal you so desire.

DAY 20

Experiencing problems is part of the natural process of life.

How you perceive them determines whether you will overcome the problems or be overwhelmed by them.

DAY 21

The race of life will always be a challenge, but no matter how you run it,

no matter how many times you trip on the hurdle or drop the baton, the

goal will always be to finish well! There is a winner in all of us.

DAY 22

Sometimes decisions are so hard when you are not sure whether you should keep something or let it go.

DAY 23

Whatever life situations you are born into are like the cards that are dealt in a card game. You have no control over either of them. In order to win at both of them, you must have a strategy that involves getting good training. Sometimes you can't get it because the instructors weren't properly trained. So you just learn by making mistakes until you master the game.

DAY 24

*One must learn never to make a
permanent decision
about a temporary situation.*

DAY 25

*The waves of life will always come.
Either you're going to learn
how to surf well or allow them to
knock you down.*

DAY 26

You must learn to control your impulses because if you don't, your impulses will definitely control you and lead you into a place where you do not want to end up.

DAY 27

It is very easy to get away from people we don't like, but it's so hard to get away from the people that we love when it's time for us to spend time alone to accomplish the things we want to do in life.

DAY 28

One of the greatest battles you will fight in your life is the battle that goes on in your mind every single day. It's a struggle to keep the right thoughts, ideas, and images in their proper perspective, especially when you still have the wrong thoughts, ideas, and images that were picked up over the years.

DAY 29

Every now and then life seems to throw us a curveball that knocks us down. We must realize that it is never about the fall, but about how we get back up and prepare ourselves for the next unexpected curveball.

DAY 30

The best solution for when you run into someone you really don't
want to deal with for whatever reason, is just keep it moving.

DAY 31

Perseverance is the ability not to give up or give in, no matter what life throws at you.

DAY 32

Sometimes it is so difficult to walk away from a difficult situation because we don't want to hurt the person or feel hurt, but we know that staying in the relationship is no good for us. It's better to be free than to grow bitter for not doing what we know is the right thing to do.

DAY 33

When someone does something that really hurts us, the easiest

things to do is to be silent, give him or her a nasty attitude, blow up on him or her

or avoid them altogether, but the hardest thing to do is confront

the person to resolve the issue.

DAY 34

Temptation is something we all battle daily, whether the desire is right or wrong. If we know it's wrong, we should try to resist it, and if it's right, we should be careful not to try to get what we want by using the wrong method.

DAY 35

Living a life of integrity is difficult, and it's hard to be consistent at times.

It means to do what's right when no one is looking; to do what's right when everyone is looking to do wrong; to be willing to do what's not popular in a popular culture; to stand firm in your convictions and not compromise under pressure; and, finally, to stand up for God when others are afraid to.

DAY 36

Life consists of a series of tests that we pass, fail, or repeat. We never really know how much strength we have down in us until we have been confronted with that difficult test which was designed to crush us but we managed to conquer and come out on top.

DAY 37

I believe the easy way is not always the best way, but the greater the difficulty, the greater the growth

DAY 38

When you know you need to do something in your heart but are a bit hesitant because of your feelings, just do it. Your feelings are real, but they aren't always right,

and decisions made off of emotions tend to cause a lot of problems.

DAY 39

Don't always resist the hard situations because you will never know

what you had in you until you met the challenge and overcame it.

DAY 40

Change is a part of life. You may not like it; you may not want

to accept it; but either way, you have to deal with it.

DAY 41

Change is necessary for growth within your life, and until you are uncomfortable with your situation, the change cannot take place.

DAY 42

Change brings criticism, and when you decide to change for the better,

you will learn who your friends are and who they are not.

DAY 43

Where you are in life is the result of your choices, no one else's,

and if you don't like where you are, you don't have to stay there

DAY 44

There is always a reason for the season and the transition to be

repositioned. How a person handles the change determines

whether he or she would come out better than before.

DAY 45

One thing you must realize is that when you know you've changed for the better, you don't have to prove anything to anyone. Just live and let your life speak for itself because, this I know about people, they will always remember you from the last image they held of you, and it can be from twenty years ago.

DAY 46

When you learn to accept that some things will never change, which
includes people, you will realize that life gets so much easier.

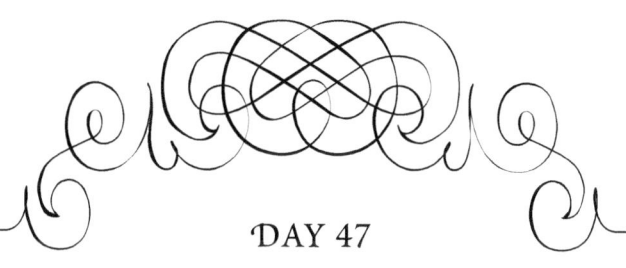

DAY 47

I believe the reason people go through the same stuff continuously every year is they refuse to change, yet they expect different results when they make the same choices.

The only way that things are going to change is to get better information. So whatever you choose to feed your mind is what you're going to produce, and you shouldn't get mad if you're in the same place next year.

DAY 48

One change people must make in their lives is to sever ties with those people who are unnecessary constant irritations. They tend to have a negative outlook on life, they are very critical of others, they are self-centered, and they have all the answers, yet their lives are a mess. We tolerate them to spare their feelings, but I say to let them go-even if they are family.

DAY 49

One thing that makes a diamond precious is that it survives the intense pressure and heat of the process to become that beautiful gem. So it is

with many of us who survived going through the process of the storms

and pressures of life, resulting in that precious gem in God's eyes.

DAY 50

People decide to embrace change when they are uncomfortable with their present state and are ready to admit something is wrong.

DAY 51

Sometimes when God changes the seasons in our lives, we miss the switch

and suffer the consequences for staying in the old season too long.

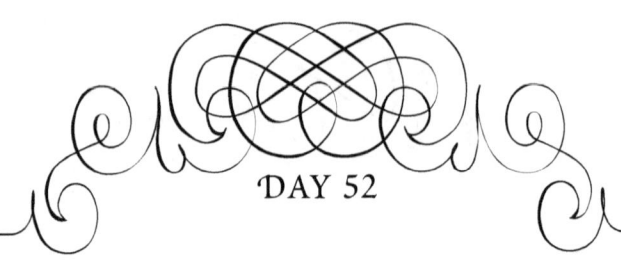

DAY 52

There are so many people who are not satisfied with where they are in life, yet they do absolutely nothing to change their position. They criticize others for being better, for doing better, and for acquiring things that their money could buy. They want so many things and want to live a certain lifestyle but fail to understand that their income can only grow to the extent that they do. In order to grow, they must change and if they don't want to change, then they won't grow.

DAY 53

Your life is like a remote, and you're in control. If you don't like what you're seeing, then change the channel until you're satisfied.

DAY 54

Change is going to happen and once the process begins, you can't control it. So you either are going to master it or become a victim of it.

DAY 55

When you are sure and secure about who you are within your own skin, you will congratulate and not hate; you won't just accept anything, and you won't tolerate abuse in any form from anyone. You will stand strong when others are long gone.

DAY 56

Never settle for less when you deserve to have so much more. Treat yourself as a priority, so others won't treat you as an option!

DAY 57

Really confident people have no need to toot their own horns, they don't brag about their successes or what they have, they don't put others down to make themselves look good, and, most important, they don't take credit for what they didn't do.

DAY 58

I have learned it is not what people say about me, but what God says about me that matters. In my faith, God says that I'm the head, not the tail, above, not beneath, and I'm more than a conqueror. When I look over my life and see what he has carried me through, "I agree with Hezekiah Walker "God favored Me." He's giving me double for all my trouble and restoring all the years I wasted through ignorance.

DAY 59

God never created us to lose; He created us to win in life and live life more abundantly. So no matter what's going on, this is what God desires for all of his children.

DAY 60

As I continue to grow and reposition myself to receive better things in life, I constantly remind myself that I don't owe the hood or anyone anything. I have not forgotten my roots, but that is not who I am today nor will I ever apologize for becoming a better person and living a better quality of life.

DAY 61

When people tell you that some things aren't possible, you have to believe within yourself that all things are possible with God.

DAY 62

While people waste their time judging your performance through life, just focus on your outcomes and let your continuous success prove the underachievers wrong.

DAY 63

Learn from your mistakes, live with no regrets, never apologize for being who you are, and live your life to the fullest.

DAY 64

You cannot allow people to kill your confidence with their insecure, controlling ways. Stay true to and stand for what you believe, and keep on speaking boldly.

DAY 65

Jealousy and envy can never rest in the heart of people who understand who they are, know that they don't have to compete with others, and accepts what God has for them is only for them.

DAY 66

Now I finally understand why people mistake other people's confidence for conceit and always say, "She or he thinks they're all that.." It is because they lack confidence and security within themselves and they do not understand it, which makes it easier to criticize others instead of focusing on themselves and doing some soul-searching to build their own confidence.

DAY 67

One of the most difficult things in life is to accept there are very few things we can control outside of ourselves.

DAY 68

It is true that the most difficult people to deal with are those who are out of control, whose sole focus is to try to control everyone else through manipulation.

DAY 69

When people constantly do things on impulse, it just reveals that they are out of control, lack discipline, and don't like structure.

DAY 70

Credibility and consistency go hand in hand. Your credibility is built up over time, and it starts with being consistent in your actions. Let's be real—people are easily disappointed, and no one likes to deal with people who can't keep their word.

DAY 71

If you don't value your word, then you shouldn't expect others to value it either.

DAY 72

Our destiny is the plan God has laid out for our lives. Sometimes we recognize it early on or a little later in life. Either way, if you don't like where your life is headed, you're the only one who can change your destiny.

DAY 73

If you find your passion, you will discover your purpose, and you will enjoy your life doing what you love to do.

DAY 74

Don't waste your precious time. Make your life count. God didn't put you here for nothing. Discover your purpose, and if you don't know it, then ask God to reveal it to you.

DAY 75

God always has the best plan for your life, and he leaves it up to you to find it. The moment you discover your passion, you've discovered your purpose and God's plan will unfold.

DAY 76

Your history is not your destiny. People may know you from way back in the day, but it's all about today and where you're headed.

DAY 77

Go-getters in life are allergic to complacency and complaining.

They never sweat the competition, they are confident in their abilities,

and they do what it takes to make their dreams come true.

DAY 78

A dream to do something in life is the same process as pregnancy. It starts out as a thought. Then it's conceived; it must be carried; it might be complicated; it also can be miscarried because of things inside of you; it can be aborted for whatever reason or you can persevere until God's appointed time and give birth through the help of others. A dream delayed is not a dream denied.

DAY 79

So many people have dreams to become something or do something Special, but what they never anticipated is what happens in between the actual dream and the fulfillment of the dream. This is because life is filled with many twists and turns that often cloud our vision, but I encourage you to keep on pushing forward in the face of adversity and watch God make your dreams come true.

DAY 80

I have learned to be on the lookout for dream killers who are out to assassinate dreams and kill the hope one has for one's future.

DAY 81

Dreams do come true as long as you believe and allow God to build your dream team,

because he knows who is the best qualified people to help you accomplish your dreams. So some people will have to suffer rejection if they are not a divine connection.

DAY 82

Moving toward making your dreams happen is serious business because you have to be on the lookout for team haters who deeply envy you and want to get close to you so they can attempt to steal your secrets and sabotage all that you worked hard for.

DAY 83

Behind every successful person, there is a group of unsuccessful people who lack the focus to make their own dreams come true.

DAY 84

Sometimes this race in life can make you weary to the point that you don't want to jump over the hurdles anymore, but I encourage you to keep on running and look to God for your strength because one thing I know is that the race isn't over until God says it's over, and in his eyes we are all winners.

DAY 85

What God has for you is for you. Don't allow anyone to deter you from your purpose and from pursuing your dream. He is the one who planted it in your heart, and it is he who will make it come to pass. Just keep him first and don't forget to give God all the glory.

DAY 86

Every day when we wake up, we never know what the day is going to be like. Sometimes we encounter challenges that are very difficult to bear or that persistent issue that doesn't seem as if it is ever going to go away, but I encourage you to stand strong, pray, and put your trust in God. For the battle is not yours, it's the Lord's. If you can remember this, it will make your day a little more peaceful.

DAY 87

You never know how much strength you have until God allows you to go through the fire, to experience a severe trial, or to be persecuted beyond comprehension. Just know that there is a purpose in everything you go through and that God has built you in a way that you will never break.

DAY 88

The only person who knows you better than yourself is God. He knows where he brought you from, where you are at now, and where he's taking you. On some days he will hold your hand, and sometimes he will carry you through the storm. So be encouraged. You have to do what's best for you and live your life without worrying about what people think and making no apologies at all.

DAY 89

People will always criticize what they don't understand, and that's something they have to take up with God. Be proud of who you are and how far you have come, and know that you're more than a conqueror. Stay focused and know that the best is yet to come.

DAY 90

When you come to realize that no experience should ever be wasted and that one season of your life prepares you for another, there is nothing you can't achieve, and you can't be stopped.

DAY 91

Success is determined by dedication, hard work, motivation, and sacrifice. And that is the major difference between those who make it happen for themselves and those who watch things happen for others.

DAY 92

I'm a firm believer that there is no recession with God. If you have the faith to believe and move forward, he'll make things happen for you that will have other people wondering.

DAY 93

I have learned that life is not fair, but God is. He's not like people who often leave you and forsake you when you need them the most. He can be trusted, he won't tell your business, and with him by your side you have nothing to fear.

DAY 94

Be inspired and motivated to do that thing you always wanted to do, and do not worry about what other people think. As long as you have breath, it's never too late.

DAY 95

To be challenged in life is inevitable. To be defeated is optional. Live your life every day with a winning attitude and you'll see the victory in every situation.

DAY 96

When God opens a door, no man can shut it, and when God shuts a door, no man can open it

DAY 97

I realize that many people are afraid to fail, but I tell you that failure can be the greatest source of motivation, and here is something to ponder, "Every person who has ever done great things has failed along the way."

DAY 98

Purpose-driven people understand that failure is a part of the process to achieve success.

DAY 99

When you view your failures as stepping stones to success, you will view your mistakes as mini-miracles.

DAY 100

Some people just don't realize that they block their own success because they think too much and focus on some of the wrong things.

DAY 101

If you have faith and step out on it, then you will realize that you can only do your best, and God will take care of the rest.

DAY 102

The only difference between the impossible and the possible is a choice and determination. Trust me when I say that you will never know what you can have until you step out on faith. Another day, another opportunity.

DAY 103

If you expect great things, then great things will happen, and sometimes God requires that we let go of something so we can receive bigger and better things that he knows we can handle.

DAY 104

To have faith means to believe in what I can't see, to take the one step and God will definitely take care of the rest while showing the world that what it said was impossible is always possible with him.

DAY 105

When you believe in the invisible, you can do the impossible.

DAY 106

Family is a subject that can be difficult to talk about for some because what family means to one person doesn't mean the same to others.

DAY 107

As the saying goes, "A house divided against itself cannot stand," and many things may have caused the division. One person cannot fix what has been broken for generations. That person can only work on himself or herself and recognize the new family God has given him or her.

DAY 108

Growing up in a family can be such a challenge with so many diverse personalities.

DAY 109

I have come to realize that you can be raised around family most of your life, and just when you think you know them, something will take place that lets you know that you didn't know them at all. We have all witnessed or read about a family member who has betrayed a family member quicker than his or her own worst enemy.

DAY 110

The lies that some family members tell and the things they cover up can damage many lives, not only in their generation but the ones coming behind them. Truth is needed always.

DAY 111

I am so glad that I grabbed ahold of the promise that God gave Abraham in Genesis 12:1–3 about leaving his home and family because he was going to bless him and make his name great. The way I understand it, is that although he had to leave them physically, he also had to leave behind the thoughts, ideas, and mindset that didn't agree with God's.

DAY 112

All families have flaws and issues, but how they manage them determines whether the family unit is healthy or unhealthy.

DAY 113

*Don't allow fear to control your life. For God did not give us a spirit of Fear. He gave us a spirit of love, power, and a sound mind. Call out that fear, confront that fear, and, finally, conquer that fear.
You can do it!*

DAY 114

*Fear is nothing but
False Evidence Appearing Real.
It is a powerful force that has the ability
to paralyze the mind, shut you down, and
literally steal your life from you.*

DAY 115

Fear is a natural condition of the mind that causes you to meditate on something that didn't even happen yet.

DAY 116

Forgiving others is a subject that many people avoid because once they feel they have been hurt or have perceived they have been hurt, they want person who hurt them to feel hurt the way they do.

DAY 117

Forgiveness is not optional, but mandatory, to maintain your health.

DAY 118

Forgiving people is one of the hardest things to do, especially when your mind never lets you forget the offense. What helps me forgive the person is the fact that God has forgiven me for all my mess, and what I choose to do is change my attitude toward the memory and move on freely.

DAY 119

To harbor unforgiveness is to arrest your emotions and to live in a mental prison without walls. To be free, you must use the keys of letting go, moving on, and not looking back.

DAY 120

People can commit an act toward you with impure motives that they know are wrong and unwittingly end up self-imprisoned because of it. Sometimes it takes the person who was wronged to be the bigger person and release the other person. It's hard, but it's a necessary thing to do if you practice forgiveness.

DAY 121

Wounding is an event, healing is a process, and forgiveness is not optional. In my faith, I'm comforted and released from all the guilt just by knowing that God has forgiven me for all that I have done past, present, and future. This is why I let go and let God.

DAY 122

For God has taught me that in order to truly love someone, I must have forgiven everyone.

DAY 123

Forgiving those who hurt us is hard to do, but it's necessary for us to have peace of mind. As long as we don't forgive them, they have more power over our minds than we do.

DAY 124

Unforgiveness is toxic to your soul, and if you don't let it go, you can end up only harming yourself. So while you're so busy nursing your wound and talking about the offense, the person is living his or her life, not thinking about you.

DAY 125

Many people use the term friend loosely, without understanding the meaning of what a true friend is. This is why so many people end up betrayed and hurt when they thought someone was a real friend, but all along the person was actually just a superficial association with no depth to the relationship.

DAY 126

Sometimes God will allow some of our friends to come along with us on our journey, and there are some friends who aren't supposed to go along for the ride.

DAY 127

I believe that to have good friends, you must first be a good friend.

DAY 128

True friends are a rare commodity, and you don't have to look for them ever. They find you.

DAY 129

Through his life, Jesus taught the greatest lesson on friendship and trust. He chose to walk with twelve but only three of them he allowed to be his friends that he could entrust his heart to, even though he knew that they would fall short. He also taught that within the crowd there will always be that Judas who will get close enough to you but always end up hanging himself because he never truly shared the same heart as you.

DAY 130

I believe that all relationships must go through an extensive interview process, especially friendships. We must do a whole lot of listening and a lot less talking, so that way we can determine if the individual is a seasonal acquaintance or a qualified one who is worthy to be in our inner circle.

DAY 131

Your true friends will love you unconditionally; they will catch you when you fall; they believe the best for you and encourage the best in you; they understand your deepest concerns; celebrate your successes, and share your pain; they pull you up when you are in the wrong; and, most important. they will never cut you off when there is a difference in opinion.

DAY 132

There's nothing like having those people in your circle who appreciate you for who you are and not for what you can do for them.

DAY 133

A crisis will show you who your friends are and who they are not.

DAY 134

Sometimes when your friends are going through a crisis, they don't necessarily want you to fix their problem. They may just want the assurance that you are there and that they have your ear.

DAY 135

A true friend never has to tell you he or she is a friend.

DAY 136

A true, loyal friend will walk through the storms with you and will even hold the umbrella for you when you can't.

DAY 137

Real friends will tell you what you need to hear, not what you want to hear. They won't always agree with you, and they will hold you accountable for your actions. If you have surrounded yourself with people who cannot follow through with these things, then it's time for a change.

DAY 138

God is love and God loves us even when we do not love ourselves at times. He never leaves us nor forsakes us. When we are weary and tired from the complexities of this thing we call life, he often carries us when we don't have the strength to carry ourselves.

DAY 139

God's love assures us that if he is for us, it doesn't matter who comes against us. God is our shield and protector, and as long as he's in the midst, nothing else shouldn't matter.

DAY 140

When we are heading for trouble, God will often send us a little warning sign that we often see, but we choose to ignore. Then he'll be courteous enough to send another one that he makes sure we won't ignore because of his mercy for us not to experience unnecessary consequences of a choice that we have made.

DAY 141

Trust God, he won't disappoint. He's there for you when people walk away, and his love is unconditional.

DAY 142

Without God, I am nothing, and because there is a God, I know who I am today, where I am, what I'm doing, how I'm doing it, and why I'm doing it.

For God loved me when I didn't love myself, he believed in me when I didn't

Believe, and he picked me up when life beat me down.

DAY 143

One thing we must learn to do is to appreciate the good supportive people in our lives who are open-minded. They are the ones who will tell us what we need to hear, not what we want to hear, and they refuse to cosign our mess.

DAY 144

I'm just grateful for both my victories and setbacks throughout life, which resulted in me living, learning, and then moving on.

DAY 145

I have learned to appreciate the moment that God chose to reveal himself to me. This is why I never say that I found God because God was never lost. I was. He has been faithful to me as I walked in my foolish ways. He never stopped loving me when I wasn't loving myself. He guided me through every fall and picked me up so I could stand tall and praise his mighty name.

DAY 146

This is one of the true statements in life: "You can only be responsible for your own happiness and not others because you can never please people because they are never satisfied."

DAY 147

To be happy is a personal choice, and one of the best ways to be happy is to start looking within and then start getting rid of all the unhappy people in your life.

DAY 148

Show me a happy person, and I will show someone who didn't waste his or her time with unhappy people, places, or things.

DAY 149

If you're smiling on the inside, then you will be smiling on the outside. Now that's what happiness is all about.

DAY 150

People are responsible for their own happiness, and the quickest way for you to become unhappy is trying to keep others happy.

DAY 151

We have only one life to live, and how it turns out is solely determined by us. How we are remembered is based on the decisions that we make and the reality is that someone will always be affected by our choices. Personally, I work hard on correcting the things I have done wrong that had a negative impact on people because my name is all I have, and I want to leave a good legacy behind.

DAY 152

You will never know you made a difference in someone's life until they tell you, and when they do, it's a beautiful feeling.

DAY 153

In life, you never get a second chance to make a first impression. So it's important to be mindful of our ways and actions at all times because you never know who you will meet that could help you get to the next level in life.

DAY 154

Jealousy means the fear of being replaced and envy means to want what someone has. They are both deeply rooted in competitive spirits of people who do not realize who they really are in God's eyes, don't realize God created them to be an original with their own gifts/talents, and they don't realize that what God has for them is just for them.

DAY 155

Insecure people tend to feel secure only when they believe they have control over something.

DAY 156

Insecure people are always intimidated by confident individuals.

DAY 157

Insecurity in any relationship is the fastest way for it to dissolve.

DAY 158

Acquiring knowledge is meaningless when you don't have the wisdom to skillfully apply that knowledge.

DAY 159

To educate a man and mind without morals is to produce a threat to society who will not accept or take responsibility for his actions; have disregard for human life, and live a life guided by the code of the streets, which will ultimately result in physical, mental, and spiritual death.

DAY 160

Too much knowledge can lead to so much confusion.

DAY 161

The best leaders are the ones who failed along the way, made mistakes, learned from them, and aren't afraid to be transparent and share their mistakes with others.

DAY 162

Being a leader is never easy, and there isn't one great leader who wasn't a follower first.

DAY 163

The greatest leaders and bosses are the ones who have not forgotten that they were once subordinates. Those who have forgotten become power struck as well as controlling, and abuse is inevitable, and the people suffer.

DAY 164

An ineffective leader is a leader who does not have his ego in check.

DAY 165

If you profess that you are a leader and no one is following you, then you're basically taking a walk by yourself.

DAY 166

Effective leaders are innovators and motivators.

DAY 167

If you fail to learn, then you have learned how to fail, and you will never reach your full potential

DAY 168

As soon as people believe they know everything, it is a clear sign that they know nothing at all, and it reveals they don't have a teachable spirit.

DAY 169

If you are not content in your current situation and you want elevation, then seek new information that will give you a revelation into how to reach your desired destination successfully, and when all that has been achieved, it's time for celebration.

DAY 170

I would rather learn from a person who has learned from his or her mistakes than from a person who can't admit to his or her mistakes.

DAY 171

Life is nothing but a class taught by different teachers; if you fail to show up, you miss the lessons and won't be able to pass the tests that promotes you to the next higher level in life.

DAY 172

A smart person learns from his or her mistakes but a wiser person learns from someone else's mistakes.

DAY 173

God has given us a life to live, and if you haven't discovered how to live life on purpose with purpose, then ask God to reveal it to you.

DAY 174

Anyone can live life, but the question is, can he or she manage the life he or she is living?

DAY 175

*No pain, no gain. No deposit, no return.
And this is life and what you make it.*

DAY 176

Life is a race that we all run with hurdles along the way that try to stop us from reaching the finish line. Many give up after a few hurdles, but many of us trip and fall only to get back up and to run the race harder.

DAY 177

For me, living with regrets is just not cool. I don't live with regrets because if I went through it or did something, then it was meant to be. If I needed to learn a lesson, then I got it. Life is just too short for the "could've, would've" syndrome.

DAY 178

When you remember that yesterday is history and tomorrow is a mystery, you'll appreciate the gift of today and live your life on purpose and for a purpose.

DAY 179

Life is nothing but a stage play with a cast of characters and no matter what role you play, we must be prepared for the changes that each scene brings. We must perform to the best of our ability, and when it's all said and done we must bow out gracefully to the round of applause, knowing that our lives were a smash hit.

DAY 180

Life isn't really too short. It's just that many people get a late start and for so long they aren't living, they are merely existing. They waste so much time that they can never get back and now they feel that they are running out of it. Just slow down, pace yourself, and then you will be able to enjoy your life to the fullest.

DAY 181

If you are not happy with the way your life is going, then work on creating the life that you want, and you can start by speaking positive things that will eventually bring positive results to you.

DAY 182

Sometimes you just have to fall back, chill out, and be you while enjoying your life.

DAY 183

When it comes down to living this life, there are only two major options, and you're either going to be a winner who never quits or a quitter who never wins. There's no in between. The choice is yours, and no one can decide this for you.

DAY 184

I was once told that you can give without loving, but you cannot truly love without giving.

DAY 185

Some people don't realize that if you don't love yourself, then how do you have the capacity to love others and how do you expect others to love you?

DAY 186

Here are a few things that I believe will tell whether a person truly loves himself or herself: 1) See if you continuously go through the same things unnecessarily. 2) Do you allow people to talk and treat you any kind of way? 3) Do you find yourself merely existing instead of living?

DAY 187

Love is so many beautiful things, but the one thing that it's not is abusive in any form.

DAY 188

True love is a feeling that you can't really explain and is something that you don't want to live without.

DAY 189

I have learned that love is an unconditional commitment to an important person, and when that person falls short, love forgives, restores the person, and starts all over with him or her.

DAY 190

People will tell you all day that they love you, but make sure they love themselves first before you can take their words seriously because the way they treat themselves is an indication of how they will treat you.

DAY 191

Love doesn't control people, love doesn't smother people, and love certainly does not place unrealistic expectations on people either, but love does believe the best in people, love does brings the best out of people, and love does keep peace between people.

DAY 192

We shouldn't search for true love but instead be patient and let true love find us when we least expect it.

DAY 193

Love doesn't hurt, love does not abuse, and love certainly won't cause you to lose yourself trying to please someone else.

DAY 194

Love doesn't dwell on what went wrong, but, instead, love focuses on how to make things right.

DAY 195

Most people who own a car have a GPS system that they rely on to lead them to their destination when they can't get their on their own knowledge. I believe that when it comes to living this life, we also need a system that will help us navigate through the trials and tribulations to reach our destination that we so desire. I call it the "God Proof System," and it never fails. When he takes over, we become designated drivers.

DAY 196

To navigate this life really successfully, we all need a little Good Orderly Direction.

DAY 197

Sometimes we make decisions that have serious consequences because we have too much noise going on in our lives, which results in the silencing of the inner voice of our souls that God speaks through us. So anytime you know that you are experiencing some technical difficulties in your inner voice and are looking for guidance, just meditate on Psalm 46:10: "Be still and know that I'm God."

DAY 198

When one door shuts and you don't know why, trust that God already has the other one open for you to walk through.

DAY 199

I believe that any setbacks in life set you up for the greatest opportunity for a comeback.

DAY 200

What seems impossible to people is always possible with God, and when it's time for God to do a new thing in your life, he will switch the seasons and present you with an opportunity that you must do something with, and if your mind is stuck in yesterday, you will never move into what God is doing for you today.

DAY 201

So many people miss out on great opportunities because they don't recognize their own potential. If you don't step up to take an opportunity, someone else has no problem with capitalizing on your loss.

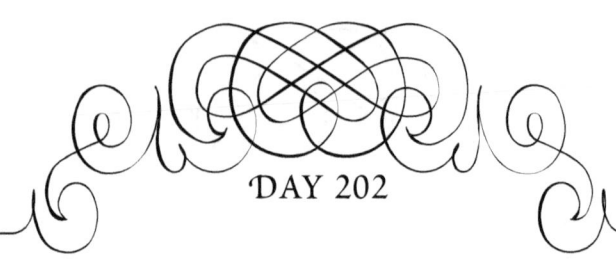

DAY 202

When driving in traffic, we will occasionally experience traffic jams, and out of frustration we try to get around it by going another way, only to run into more traffic that delays us from reaching our destination. This holds true when moving through life. We want to go through things quickly or around them altogether. The reality is that there are no shortcuts. The journey is a process to teach you life lessons, and patience is one of them.

DAY 203

Life will teach you that you can only offer your hand to help someone, but it's up to the person to grab ahold of it. Very few will take it, and many of them won't because of the fear of being disappointed, but I encourage you to be patient with them and still keep your hand extended.

DAY 204

Sometimes we make a lot of unnecessary mistakes and end up in situations that we shouldn't be in because we move too fast in life. I believe that it's better to recognize on our own to slowdown rather than life do it for us because we often don't like the results.

DAY 205

For the things you do not understand in life, try not To lose any sleep trying to figure them out.

DAY 206

Maintaining your peace should be primary in your life because, in the absence of it, chaos dwells.

DAY 207

Peace is something you work hard to obtain but don't ever want to lose.

DAY 208

Peace is that inner quality that assures you that everything is okay.

DAY 209

Sometimes people come into our lives whom we wish we had never met.

DAY 210

To know a person is to know his or her history, and if you don't know
a person's history, then you really don't know the person.

DAY 211

People will always try to put a period on your life where God already has a comma to remind them your testimony continues on, and they can't stop it.

DAY 212

Sometimes when you're going through stressful situations the person you expect to be there isn't, and the person you least expected is right there by your side. Everything happens for a reason.

DAY 213

No matter how well you treat people, there is that one person who is never satisfied and who is very ungrateful.

DAY 214

Some people's sole motive is to get close to you so they can listen for your secrets, slander your name, spread lies, and assassinate your character.

DAY 215

Sometimes the snakes are not hiding in the grass; they are in plain sight, trying to spread their poison.

DAY 216

The person who casts a stone at you will be the same one who will get hit with a boulder.

DAY 217

Be careful who you let into your life and who you become intimate with. You have to know whether the person is going to add to your life or suck the life out of you.

DAY 218

Some things are just not hidden and when people show you who they are and who they are not, please believe them.

Some things don't need to be second guessed.

DAY 219

One of the things that people must understand is that they, not others, are responsible for the motives of their own hearts. If your motives are pure, then you have nothing to worry about, nor do you have to defend your actions.

DAY 220

People will never truly get to know you until they understand where you come from, what you've been through, what you had to overcome, and how you ended up where you are today. To know you is a privilege and not a right.

DAY 221

Respect is something that people command, and it is said that in order to get respect you must give respect. That's all good, but first people must learn what respect is, and if they haven't been taught, they are only going to do what they have been doing to those who accept it.

DAY 222

Yeah, it's true that people will clap for you when you're up, stomp on you when you're down, assassinate your character, slander your name, and sell you out.

DAY 223

There are just some things in life that will never change, and this is why I often remind myself that bad company corrupts good morals, and I meditate on Psalm 1:1: "Blessed is the man that walks not in the counsel of the ungodly nor stands in the way of sinners." This is why you always have to be careful with whom you walk and talk because negativity is like cancer. It spreads rapidly and kills the goodness in you.

DAY 224

The one thing that people love to do that God will never do is tell your business.

DAY 225

If people can't get down with you when you are going through your mess, there is no way they can celebrate you as you achieve your success.

DAY 226

Some people just don't have the capacity to receive the love and kindness that you extend from the depths of your heart.

DAY 227

I strive daily to treat people with respect and kindness, but some people respond by treating me in the completely opposite way, which makes no sense at all.

DAY 228

When people attack your character, it means they are afraid of you, and they want what you have but aren't willing to do what you did to get it.

DAY 229

Some people are like the weather; they're always changing, unpredictable, and they'll disappoint you if you let them.

DAY 230

Always stay clear of a person with a suspect personality. They always look for what's wrong, they falsely accuse others when they are the ones who are doing all the dirt, and they always look to assassinate people's characters.

DAY 231

No matter how hard you try, there are just some people who don't want to let go. They want to stay relevant in your life when they've already been removed. Just keep it moving, and don't allow that pain from your past to poison your future.

DAY 232

When show love to those who hate you, bless those who curse you, and give to those who think they are using you, you will always shine bright in the midst of their darkness.

DAY 233

Just as you can be fooled by the wrappings on a gift box and what you believe is on the inside, you can be fooled by people who appear stunning on the outside, but who are quite different on the inside. So know that outer beauty can never be the basis for judging a person's character.

DAY 234

Never entertain those people who focus only on who you were in the past, don't respect who you have grown into now, and really don't care where you're headed in the future.

DAY 235

I have learned that people who are conditioned to abuse, whether it is mentally, physically, spiritually, or emotionally, are the hardest people to deal with. Their state of mind is not to be played with. They will turn your good into bad, they will make it seem like every person who comes into their lives is out to hurt them, and they try to get their way by any means necessary at the expense of others.

DAY 236

Always know that the people stuck in rewind within their own lives never want you to see you progressively move fast-forward in your own.

DAY 237

Never take advice from a person who's always talking and never has time to listen to anyone outside of himself or herself.

DAY 238

In life, perception is everything, and how you view the world and others is determined by how you see yourself and where you. are within your life.

DAY 239

If people come to realize they need to change their perspective on a lot of issues, they will see that life really can be good to them if they decide to participate in it and stop sitting on the sidelines complaining.

DAY 240

It is a great feeling when you make plans for the day, and you accomplish everything that you set out to do. I am a firm believer in the adage "If you fail to plan, then you plan to fail."

DAY 241

One thing I learned about life is that everybody ends up somewhere; however, very few people end up somewhere on purpose. Let's face it—strategic planning is the key element for a successful life, and if you are not planning, then ask yourself if you're unconsciously planning to fail. This is something that nobody wants, but, in all reality, it does happen. So if you have a plan, make sure you prepare yourself to execute it effectively.

DAY 242

God has a plan for everyone, regardless of where you are from, what you did, and how you did it. His Grace, Mercy, Forgiveness, and Love cover a multitude of sins, which frees you from living with guilt. He doesn't remember the things of your past and neither should you. Therefore, it is up to you to discover, embrace, and live out God's plan with no regrets.

DAY 243

I have learned that the greatest source of my past issues was my inner me that was destroying me, and until I learned how to love me, I could never truly love others outside of me.

DAY 244

Everyone has the potential to succeed, but many don't because they fear success, and they sabotage their own progress.

DAY 245

Throughout my life experiences, I have learned that my life is not for me but for others, and if I can help one person,

then my job is done. I believe in honesty and transparency. I am never afraid to share out of fear of gossip because no one can tell my story better than I can.

DAY 246

You cannot allow other people's unrealistic expectations to control you. Do what you believe is right for you, and do not be concerned about people being disappointed in you. You owe no one anything.

DAY 247

Don't get too caught up in praise from people because the same ones who clap for you will be the same ones who will crucify you

DAY 248

Karma can be your best friend or worst enemy, and that is something only you can decide.

DAY 249

One day people will recognize the power behind keeping most of their business to themselves. If you tell it all, then you shouldn't get mad when it's spread around, chopped up, and then some. If you don't care, don't expect the next person to care.

DAY 250

The difference between successful and unsuccessful people is their attitude and determination.

DAY 251

I am a firm believer that everyone has inside of them the potential to do great things, but it sometimes doesn't manifest because we often get in our own way by not believing in ourselves. We then reject the people who can help us reach our potential and cling to people who poison our potential.

DAY 252

Sometimes people don't realize that rejection is nothing but God's blessing in disguise. So that promotion you didn't get, that relationship that didn't work out, that deal you wanted to make, that house you didn't close on, or that car you didn't get, don't worry. God sees something you don't see, and he definitely has something way better coming down the pipeline. Be patient and hold on.

DAY 253

Every now and then, God will take us through a little R & B test. R & B means "Run it Back" and sometimes he just wants to see if we have forgotten the lesson that we learned when we went through the test the first time.

DAY 254

Just because something feels good, doesn't mean you should have it or it's the best thing for you.. Don't allow your feelings to dictate your sound judgment.

DAY 255

Everyone needs a little G.O.D (Good Orderly Direction) in his or her life. For if you do not know where you are, you certainly do not know where you are headed.

DAY 256

Those who desire to be successful will first learn the importance of getting up early, using time wisely, managing money effectively, being organized, being strategic in their planning, and being well prepared.

DAY 257

Although we like to address the ego when we talk about men, everyone has one, and when your ego is in the driver's seat in your life, it is a clear indication that you have Eased God Out, and as a small reminder, God does not take a backseat to anyone, and he will bring you back to reality as he sees fit.

DAY 258

Complaining about a situation does not change it. It just reminds you that you have a problem that needs to be fixed.

DAY 259

Many of us eventually come to realize that God has a plan for our lives and so does the devil, and when I finally decided to wake up, I hurried up and switched sides.

DAY 260

Do not be foolish and make someone a priority in your life when you already know he or she sees you as an option.

DAY 261

One thing I realize is that when you are down, the only place you can go is up, and sometimes you have to take a loss so you can gain more than you ever had and to reach new heights that you never achieved.

DAY 262

Misery loves company, and it is always looking for friends.

DAY 263

It costs you nothing to be a responsible person, but it will cost you everything if you're irresponsible.

DAY 264

I have learned by experience that experience is not the best teacher, and I refuse to go through another major life-altering situation when I do not have to. I have learned that listening is my greatest asset, and I have no problem taking advice from people who take their own and lead by example.

DAY 265

I have heard so many people joke about how they are "beating the system." However, what they need to realize is that the joke is on them. The system is designed to crush your creative ability, keep your mentality in a poor condition that produces poor thinking, and have you living in poverty-like conditions. Those who understand the systems of this world learned how to successfully navigate them and rise to the top.

DAY 266

I have learned that God doesn't help those who help themselves. He helps those who are helpless. Why do I say this? Because if we can do everything ourselves, then why do we need God's help?

DAY 267

Sometimes relationships are broken that we want to mend, and when we begin the process of mending them, we have to make sure we are mending the right one. Always examine the root causes that initially caused the separation; see what role you played; reflect back on the foundation the relationship was built upon; and then you can decide from that point whether it is an asset or a liability.

DAY 268

Sometimes you just cannot avoid dealing with toxic people on some level, but that doesn't mean you have to give them a permanent position in your life.

DAY 269

Know when it's time to walk away because sometimes you stay too long in a situation that ends up dragging you all the way down where you feel like you can't get back up.

DAY 270

Some relationships are like trying to force the wrong key into a lock. It just won't work.

DAY 271

Some people just don't know how to act when someone treats them well because they're so used to being mistreated, and they also seem not to understand why the good people don't stick around.

DAY 272

People will definitely use you if you let them. There is so much freedom in just telling them no and not feeling bad. You don't have to do what they want.

DAY 273

I have learned three things about broken relationships: 1) People never took the time to learn one another 2) People have yet to learn that both sexes communicate very differently, and 3) They had sex way too soon. We need to humble ourselves, learn to do things differently, and bring something into a relationship instead of looking to get something out of it.

DAY 274

Oftentimes in a relationship people don't say what they mean or feel because they are afraid to be vulnerable, hurt, or let down. Learn to get over your fears, be honest, and hope for the best outcome.

DAY 275

The best thing you can do for yourself is not hold on to a person who wants to walk out of your life. Trust God has someone better coming your way. So hold on.

DAY 276

Just as a car needs maintenance to prevent it from breaking down, so do relationships. You have to remember often to check up on your communication, trust, loyalty, and honesty to keep the relationship running smoothly.

DAY 277

Although we were created to be in relationship with another, the truth is we all just can't get along in the way we would like to. We often blame the other person when sometimes the issue really lies within us, and if people can't get along with themselves, then how do they expect to get along with others. Self-check is always necessary to retain and maintain healthy relationships.

DAY 278

Emotions are powerful. Either you will manage them or they will manage you. They can cause you to become unstable and lead you to damage relationships.

DAY 279

Sometimes we refuse to accept that people can't give what they don't have. We often enter into relationships bringing the baggage of unrealistic expectations that we hold the other person accountable for, and the person never even signed up for those expectations.

DAY 280

Communication is the glue to all relationships. If a person has done something that has caused you to become angry, don't sit on it too long. Process the anger first and then, at the right moment, express to the individual how you feel. For if you don't tell him or her, how can he or she prevent himself or herself from repeating the offense?

DAY 281

Being in a relationship is a full-time job with plenty of overtime, and you have to work hard to keep it healthy.

DAY 282

One of the most disheartening things that can happen in a relationship is when you have grown apart instead of growing together. You believed that person was the one—he or she was that missing piece to the puzzle—but suddenly change starts taking place. The minor arguments get more intense and eventually you don't recognize that person you are sleeping with

DAY 283

Nothing gets done alone and to achieve greatness, you must have a team mindset, which means to me, "Together Everyone Achieves More."

DAY 284

Love, Loyalty and Trust, without these three elements present in any relationship there is nothing left.

DAY 285

I always remind myself that there is nothing wrong with pulling the plug on some people, places, and things when I'm tired of being their life support. Some relationships are just never worth keeping alive.

DAY 286

I could never get with the saying, "Keep your enemies close." I think that is so crazy when you know the person does not care about you. Just think, in the time of war one camp sends a spy into the other camp to study them for the sole purpose of destroying them. One side never knowingly invites the spy into their camp to take them out, and neither should you. So this serves as a reminder to be wise and strategic in your relationships

DAY 287

You should never look for anyone to complete you when you should already be whole because two people that are halfway don't make a whole relationship.

DAY 288

When you have true love in your heart and in a relationship, you realize that it's not about you but about the other person. Anything outside of that is pure manipulation to get what you want, and when the other person wakes up, you will find yourself alone.

DAY 289

Don't sweat who left. Rejoice in who stayed, and know that God has a reason for that person not advancing into your future.

DAY 290

No relationship is ever perfect. Mistakes will be made, disagreements will take place, but when true love is present, it will override these minor irritations and will not coexist with lying, cheating, and abuse in any form.

DAY 291

Life will teach you to be careful of whom you walk and talk with because everyone who cracks a smile isn't always worth your while.

DAY 292

When it comes down to Doing You, Being You, and Loving You, you need people in your life who will be supportive of you and not jealous, envious, or threatened by you.

DAY 293

Relationships will definitely show you it's all about a partnership not a dictatorship, and if one person doesn't comprehends this, he or she will thrive off of manipulation to control every aspect of the situation, which will ultimately crush your heart and leave you asking where you went wrong.

DAY 294

If a person believes that life is all about him or her, then he or she can't possibly help others.

DAY 295

There's nothing wrong with having selfish moments in life to assess where you are, where you're headed, and where you don't want to be.

DAY 296

The drama never ceases when you encounter a selfish person who acts like a child trapped in a grown person's body, whose emotions are all over the place, and who wants you to go for that wild rollercoaster ride with him or her.

DAY 297

Sometimes you have to be the sacrificial lamb so others can live. If you don't fight for what you believe, then why believe at all?

DAY 298

One of the greatest feelings one can have is putting a smile on someone's face after a single act of kindness when he or she least expects it, without looking for anything in return for yourself.

DAY 299

Being there for someone when he or she really needs you to be and that person truly appreciating it is one of the greatest feelings a person can ever have. Acts like this show the selflessness of your character and are a living example to the person you have supported with the hopes of that person doing the same for others as you have done for him or her.

DAY 300

Let us go out each day and do our part in the big world. Let us bring hope to the hopeless; let us love the unlovely; let us be strength to those who are feeling weak; let us lend our shoulders to those who need strength; and, finally, let us thank God for waking us up each day and for giving us the ability to do these things for others.

DAY 301

I've often heard people tell others, "Just fake it until you make it," but I don't understand why they do that because those who fake it never make it.

DAY 302

Nothing scares me more than perfect people who live in a perfect world who can do no wrong and are good twenty-four seven, especially when they know that down on the inside of them, they have an evil twin just like everyone else does. I know I've got one who is trying hard to run my life and sabotage it, but this I know—if I don't feed it, it won't grow.

DAY 303

So many people do not know their value nor do they have a healthy self-image, and this is mainly because they were never taught or received positive affirmations from the people who were responsible for raising them. At one point in my life, I struggled with this, but when I started on my journey with God, I found my image and self-worth in his word through Christ.

DAY 304

I believe it's not over until God says it's over because it is never about what man says about me, but what God says about me. Man places limitations, but with God there are always unlimited possibilities. Knowing this just gives me great joy.

DAY 305

I believe if people have to announce to the world who they are, they really don't understand that they are saying that they are not sure of who they are and are seeking validation from people who really care nothing about them. What they fail to realize is that as quickly as people praise them, they will curse them in the same breath.

DAY 306

Most people make the mistake of trying to fit in when God has created them to stand out.

DAY 307

I believe when you know thyself, you will know when to sit still, be quiet, and listen to what's going on in your mind to see what needs to be eliminated and what's worthy to remain.

DAY 308

It has been said that a picture is worth a thousand words, but, in reality, it has only one true meaning. Just as people call you many things, as long as you know who you truly are, their opinion just doesn't matter.

DAY 309

In the court of opinions, it never matters what people say about you; what you believe about yourself is the final verdict.

DAY 310

Always remember to thank the people who helped you along the way in your journey.

DAY 311

We should always give thanks for being allowed to see another day that affords us the opportunity to make things right that have gone wrong, mend the relationships that have been broken, and continue to be the best person that we know how to be.

DAY 312

When I reflect on where God has brought me from, where I am now, and where I'm on my way to, I look up to heaven and give thanks. For God has truly shown me that life can be greater later, there are no limits with him, and I can accomplish whatever my heart desires.

DAY 313

One important lesson I have learned is to guard your heart with all diligence.

DAY 314

A broken heart should tell you never to give your heart away to a person who doesn't deserve it.

DAY 315

Mending a broken heart is difficult to do but worth the process when you have that loving, caring person in your life to help you restore it.

DAY 316

Never be fooled by the words that people speak when you know their actions will reveal the true intentions of their hearts

DAY 317

A broken heart is like a fresh, deep cut that takes a long time to heal from the inside out, and if you cover it up too soon with a Band-Aid, the healing process only slows down.

DAY 318

Our mind has a way of playing games with memories. We know the situation isn't good for us, yet our minds will play back a few good times, and we go running back, only to get hurt again.

DAY 319

Your quality of life is determined by the quality of your thoughts, and what you choose to feed your mind is totally up to you.

DAY 320

God will always provide a way out of a situation, but most of the time, walking away is the hardest thing to do because what we are walking away from has a hold on our minds.

DAY 322

I believe that the mind is more powerful than anything. It has the power to be your greatest asset or your greatest liability. It can be a source of strength or a source of weakness. It is the place that stores all the memories that can cause you to be happy or sad.

DAY 323

Don't waste your time trying to prove anything to anyone or entertain the chatter of the doubters. Just be who you are, live your life, and give thanks for the haters for keeping you on point because it's obvious you're doing something right if they keep focusing on you.

DAY 324

One thing I always remind myself of is, if God is for me, it really doesn't matter who comes up against me.

DAY 325

At some point, you must stop energizing your enemies. If you know they are not a part of your future plans, then stop focusing on them before they start thinking they are that important.

DAY 326

Your past is something that you cannot escape, and you must remember that it has the potential to poison or prepare you for your future. You must give it respect, keep it in check, and finally realize that it is something that you must accept.

DAY 327

There's a reason why some people from your past are not allowed to participate in your future. Don't question God about it. Just trust that he knows what he's doing, and keep it moving.

DAY 328

When people begin to realize then internalize that their past history is not their destiny; that God is not interested in where they came from but where they are going, and that when people see the worst in them, God always see the best in them, they will learn to appreciate the life they have been blessed with and make the most of it.

DAY 329

We all have experienced some form of pain in the past, and we must realize the need to let that pain go and not drag it into our future.

DAY 330

You can never drive a car forward successfully if you're always looking in the rearview mirror; so it is with life. If you're always looking back to your past you can never move forward successfully into your future. Let go, let God, and keep it moving.

DAY 331

I don't believe anyone should be ashamed of his or her past. It is what it is, you are who you are, and you are still here to tell your story better than anyone else can!

DAY 332

One thing that makes a diamond precious is that it survives intense pressure and heat of the process to become that beautiful gem. So it is with many of us who survived going through the process of the storms and pressures of life resulting in that precious gem in God's eyes.

DAY 333

Sometimes there isn't a warning when one of the storms of life shows up that you have no control over. You want to do something to make it go away, but the reality is that you can't. The storm is there for an appointed time, and all you can do is pray and trust God to bring you through.

DAY 334

In order for a seed to grow, it must be placed in the right environment and watered. Place it in the wrong environment, and it produces nothing. God has placed many seeds on the inside of us that are meant to grow us into the person that he desires and to live the abundant life, but because many of us are in the wrong environment, we can't grow to the place where God wants us to be.

DAY 335

Dark and light go hand in hand, and when we go through dark periods in our lives, we must keep on pushing until we can see the light.

DAY 336

When people figure out what life is all about and what it's not about, they won't waste so much time on things that really do not matter.

DAY 337

This is the day that the Lord has made, let us rejoice and be glad in it. For you will never get this day back, and you should make the most out of it.

DAY 338

I often hear people say that life is too short. In reality it's not that it's too short; it's just that people wait too long to get started because they didn't understand that time waits for no one. Once they understand this truth, they will walk away from the people, places, and things that steal their time and prevent them from living a productive life.

DAY 339

Many people struggle with trusting other people, which causes them not to form good, solid relationships. The truth of it all is that trust begins and ends with the individual. If you can't trust yourself and know that you aren't a trustworthy person, you will never be able to trust other people.

DAY 340

Be mindful of whom you allow to speak into your life when you are in a low emotional state because people will say things that can lead you to make decisions you may regret afterwards.

DAY 341

You have to learn how to choose your battles wisely. For you don't always have to jump in the ring to fight. Some fights are for God to handle, and he certainly doesn't need fifteen rounds for the victory when he gets first-round knockouts.

DAY 342

I believe that people cannot love until they have learned to trust people, and they cannot trust them until they take the time to get to know them.

DAY 343

There is never a need to question God about where he wants to take you—just follow his lead and know it will be in your best interests.

DAY 344

Never give away your trust too fast to people, but make them work hard to earn it because betrayal is a matter of the heart, and it never shows itself up front.

DAY 345

Loyalty is loyalty. Either you're loyal or you're not. There is no in between, and those who try to play the in between will hang themselves, just like Judas.

DAY 346

Never share your personal life with a person who can't seem to connect the dots in his or her own.

DAY 347

It's better to stand alone in truth than in the presence of a crowd of people who live and tell lies.

DAY 348

One thing I have learned in life is that it is so easy to tell a lie to save face and to please people but so hard to tell the truth to maintain your integrity and stand alone for what you know is the right thing to do.

DAY 349

Remember to try to be kind to others, for you never know who God will bless you through.

DAY 350

It's better to tell the truth to keep a clear conscience rather than exhaust all that energy trying to maintain a lie that will torment your mind.

DAY 351

Loyalty can only be understood and appreciated by those who are loyal to others.

DAY 352

You can never begin a new chapter in your life if you keep rereading the previous ones. Some things you must change, including some of the characters, to make things more interesting and exciting.

DAY 353

The truth will always stand tall in a pack of lies, and when you deny the truth, you deny yourself freedom of the mind.

DAY 354

When God is ready to bless you, no one can stop it.

DAY 355

If you have no education, you have no power, and people can handle you any way that they want to.

DAY 356

You cannot push someone up the ladder if he or she does not want to take steps, just as you can't expect someone to succeed at anything if he or she is not motivated.

DAY 357

The keys to success are discipline and managing money. You can't have one without the other.

DAY 358

The sweetest revenge is Karma, but the greatest revenge is your success.

DAY 359

Success begins the moment you separate yourself from people who cannot lead you to where they have never been and you start following someone who can lead and direct you to where you want to be.

DAY 360

At times it can be difficult to enjoy the work you love to do, especially when you are overworked, underpaid, and unappreciated.

DAY 361

Integrity is doing what's right when no one is looking, to do what's right when it doesn't feel right, and to do what's right when many people around you are looking to do what's wrong, especially at work. The pressure is always intense to go with the flow, but there is nothing like the feeling when you can sleep well at night, knowing you made the right decision.

DAY 362

We often have to deal with hostile elements at work, such as office politics, gossip, out of control bosses, and secret service, double-agent coworkers who do whatever it takes to reach the top. It is enough to produce high levels of stress, but I encourage you to do your best and let God handle the rest.

DAY 363

If you ever have to switch jobs, and you remain in the same profession, understand that it's a new system and your preexisting knowledge should be on reserve. Brown-nosing with management to try to prove that you know it all without learning their system will result in you hanging yourself and receiving a not-so-pretty pink slip.

DAY 364

If you have a big dream in your heart to do your own thing and you're an employee, start thinking and moving like a boss, and eventually you will become one.

DAY 365

All I know is that true promotion comes from God in his timing.

Thank you for reading and for your support.
I encourage you to post your feedback at
www.facebook.com/RealTalkOnABlessedDay
or e-mail me at sromainp@yahoo.com.

www.ingramcontent.com/pod-product-compliance
Lightning Source LLC
LaVergne TN
LVHW051822080426
835512LV00018B/2680